COST CONSCIOUSNESS IN THE WORKPLACE

FOCUSING ON THE BOTTOM LINE AS AN EMPLOYEE

Workplace cost consciousness is every team member's responsibility from the bottom to the top. Being cost conscious helps your organization save money and ultimately stay in business over the long run. In this course, you will learn about how employees can contribute to cost control efforts by spending the organization's money wisely, including expenditures related to travel and entertainment, supply, vendor and facility costs.

DOING YOUR PART WITH COST CONSCIOUSNESS

As the saying goes, "A penny saved is a penny earned." As an employee, you can and should do your part to help your company save a penny, maybe many pennies. This is where cost management, controlling costs over the long-term comes in. Think about it, even though your organization may be successful and doing well financially, it doesn't mean that the current situation is guaranteed to last.

Circumstances in the marketplace can change very quickly. You might say they can turn on a dime. That's why it's important for companies companies to spend their money wisely to protect their earnings, so they can stay afloat during an economic downturn or when it faces a rough patch. A company spending more than it earns creates financial stress and ultimately is not sustainable. So controlling costs is a high priority activity for every organization.

One way, a company can build cost consciousness within the organization is to make all the employees feel like they matter and they're all part of a team, working towards a common goal. With everyone on the same page, the company can be confident confident that employees are working toward their goals, while employees can be confident that the company values and cares about their work, although the needs of the company and the employee may never perfectly overlap.

The more that they do, the easier it will be to meet and surpass their goals. All employees should know the profit potential of their tasks and the impact of their actions on an organization's fiscal health. For example, what are the implications of using an extra $100 a month on supplies? At first glance, this may not seem like a significant expense to an employee or a business owner, but it adds up to an extra $1200 per year that could be drawing interest in the bank or funding important growth initiatives for the business.

Employees always need to consider the opportunity costs and tradeoffs associated with their expenditures. When employees work together with the company to reduce costs, it can actually have positive long-term effects for all the employees. For example, an employee can gain valuable experience while working to help the company achieve its goals. This experience could be the launching pad to grabbing an opportunity to advance their career.

For its part, the company benefits not only from the savings, but also from from an experienced workforce that keeps one eye on expenditures at all times. It's a win-win.

GETTING STARTED ON SAVINGS

Think about it. You wouldn't intentionally waste your own money or knowingly make bad financial decisions. Why would you do it with company money? As an employee, you have a personal responsibility when it comes to spending company money. Treat it as if it were your own. Ask yourself, if this was my money, would I make the same decision and consider the full value of the money spent. In other words, is it only just about the numbers? Often, it's not.
It's also about being financially responsible and ensuring that the money is spent wisely. As a consumer, think about your own approach to pricing. For example, if you're buying a table, you may be happy to assemble it yourself at home, if you know you're saving some of your hard earned dollars. Apply the same principles principles when spending company money.
Think about the phrase, time is money. Simply put, time is valuable and shouldn't be wasted. It can be put to productive use. The less complex the task, the faster it gets done. Saving productive time saves money. Consider the basic needs and processes of your company and tighten them where you can. Keep meeting short and efficient. Reduce response times that leave people sitting and waiting.
Remember to keep tasks simple. Simpler tasks are cheaper. Complex tasks require additional time and cost to complete. Look for ways to streamline your tasks and processes. Are you generating five reports when one consolidated report would suffice? That alone frees up extra hours in the work week. Productively used,

this time might even enable the company to move work back to internal teams that's currently currently being performed by outside contractors at added expense.

Pay attention to quality from the start, so that you don't have to fix problems later. Avoid the costs incurred through warranty claims, recalls or losses. This also eliminates the need for a bloated quality control department. Employees can make a substantial contribution by increasing their productivity. For example, they can reduce the amount of time spent, checking emails or needless duplication of paperwork.

When you use tools such as instant messaging and file sharing, you can speed processes up and reduce the need for meetings and phone calls. Look for low-hanging fruit, issues and processes that are quick and cheap to address without management's involvement. Cutting waste and implementing lean processes saves productive time and therefore money. Purchasing isn't just a matter of picking the option with the smallest price tag. Consider the hidden or additional costs.

A cheaper base price doesn't always mean the cheaper total cost. Consider things like the shipping time and cost of customs or duty fees when buying from outside the country. Other hidden costs could include sales tax, delivery charges and installation, acquisition and disposal fees.

Take the total cost of ownership, TCO, the purchasing fee plus the operations costs into consideration. For instance, what is the long term cost of a company car once you include things like gas and insurance? When you're travelling, consider additional charges for in-room internet fees at hotels, checked baggage fees and rental car insurance. Managers are directly accountable for cost management, but treating company money like your own is part of everyone's job.

SAVING ON TRAVEL AND ENTERTAINMENT COSTS

Need to save some company money quick? Simple. Cut out all that spending on travel and entertainment, but wait. Sometimes, those expenses are justified. Suppose, you want to land a big out of town client, a personal visit might just seal the deal. The point is, you can't simply eliminate these costs, but you can manage them effectively to get the most benefit from the smallest outlay. If you have to travel, consider driving or taking the train instead of flying.

Save on costs by travelling together with other team members on the same day and share car pool or hotel room expenses. Where it's an option, stay with friends. Find ways to cut down on incidentals where possible, avoid luggage fees by packing light and only taking carry-on luggage or making use of the hotel shuttle to get to your accommodation, instead of a cab. Make sure you're familiar with your company's meal compensation policy and stick to it.

Weigh the pros and cons of having a company car. If a car is necessary, compare prices between car rental agencies and think about the model you really need. A car that is only for employee's use and not for shuttling clients doesn't need to be big or impressive. It's in your company's best interest to shop around for low cost deals and packages.

Take the time to look for travel packages that are all inclusive and cover things like flight, hotel and car rental. Look for the cheapest flights and consider discount airlines where available. Keep in mind that connecting flights are often cheaper than flying direct that savings can apply based on the time of the day or day of the week.

Use comparison sites such as Expedia, Priceline and Orbitz. Your company may have a list of approved vendors or in-house resources. If so, make use of them. Perhaps, there's a company account for frequent flyer miles. If your company doesn't already have one, set one up that all employees can access and establish a pool of miles to use for future travel and check with hotels and car rental agencies for any discount rates available for members of particular organizations like professional associations.

Travelling is expensive and is often easy cut to make. With established customers, consider video conferencing instead of face to face meetings. Simply avoid it when you can. But if you can't, then add more value to your trip. Try to make it more effective by meeting with additional customers at your destination.

If you're attending a conference, plan carefully. You can reduce the costs, hotels, food, car rentals by arriving late or leaving early if you don't need to attend the entire conference and take the items you need such as your laptop and charger with you. Occasional travel and entertainment are necessary expenses, but a little effort and cost management will save your company money.

SAVING ON SUPPLY COSTS

Buying supplies can't be avoided, but it needn't cost an arm and a leg. By shopping around and examining how you purchase and use them, you can routinely save on supply costs. First, shop around. It's like going to the grocers, compare prices, look for deals, try the samples, see what best fits your needs and budget, plan your spending ahead and streamline inventory management. There's even software available for this.

Where possible, buy in bulk. High volume purchases often mean increased discounts and even bogo type offers. Buying many of your supplies from the same vendor may also qualify you for discounts as well as saving time by reducing the number of vendors you have to deal with. Additionally, it increases your power with your vendor and expand your thinking to include things like health insurance and software supplies. Shop around for the best rates on insurance plans and employee benefits packages. Use free versions of software where possible. You can also save money when acquiring company equipment.

Consider a second hand option where possible and check classified ads going out of business sales and community boards like Craigslist, but you need to verify the equipment's quality. Otherwise, it may cost you more in the long run. Additionally, instead of buying, you can choose to rent or lease your equipment, especially for large ticket items such as photocopiers. Ensure that you first weigh up the cost versus benefits.

One, for example, other maintenance costs compared to purchasing it? Other ways to cut costs include reusing supplies where possible, reuse old file folders by simply changing the labels, reuse old boxes for storage or outgoing shipments, reuse packing material or sell it to other companies. Shredded non-confidential documents make great packing material. You can also pick up supplies instead of having them delivered. Identify further ways to reduce supplies and reduce waste disposal.

For example, make sure people don't have free access to supplies and aren't hoarding them. Allocate them and lock them up in a supply closet if necessary. Stick to the same equipment brand and have someone on staff learn basic troubleshooting for office equipment to reduce or avoid maintenance costs. You can also refill in cartridges and ensure that printing is double sided. Another way to save on supply costs is by going increasingly electronic.

Avoid unnecessary printing, mailing and faxing. Opt instead to store documents electronically and scan and email for delivery. You could also save on costs by buying online. The expense of office supplies might seem insignificant, but left unchecked, the costs pile up and cut into your organization's profit margin. Careful cost management applies everywhere.

SAVING ON VENDOR COSTS

Dealing with vendors is part of doing business. Cost management requires that you manage your vendor relationships to get the best deals possible. Negotiating with vendors is crucial to cost saving. Review your vendors and vendor agreements regularly to ensure they're still meeting your overall needs and that they are competitive. Then, renegotiate early and often.

Don't commit to long term price agreements for things that usually get cheaper over time like electronic equipment. Ask your vendors for perks, such as free extended warranties and make sure you get the discounts you've been promised. You can also negotiate breaks on the terms of a deal if necessary.

You can negotiate pretty much anything. Your vendor should work to earn your business, but bear in mind, you want to foster solid working relationships with vendors. It's important to negotiate yes, but appreciate that they need to make a profit too. Be reasonable about price and terms. Shop wisely for vendors, find vendors that offer that offer multiple services, so that you deal with fewer of them.

Consolidating vendors allows you more time to deal with those you do have and assures less variation in quality. You'll also buy more from them, which equals better prices. Avoid sticking to the same vendors out of habit and relationships that aren't working out and make sure that you are regularly assessing new vendors in the marketplace. Determine how important you are to your vendor and how important they are to you.

Mutually beneficial relationships seek ways both parties can win.

If they're important to you, but you're not to them, find someone who'll value your business. Consider the impact of each vendor's product or service on your bottom line. You might need to alter your agreement or eliminate the vendor altogether. Ask yourself how doing so would affect your business. For instance, make greater use of email rather than hiring couriers.

If you need to ship goods, shop around for the lowest cost provider. Often, price is determined by size, speed and distance of the shipment. Analyze this for each shipment. Do the same with things like insurance. Shop around and make sure you aren't paying for anything twice. For example, if your building's insurance covers its contents as well, then you don't need to insure office equipment separately.

Make it a point to review your policies carefully and make sure you aren't unnecessarily wasting money. And why pay to use others' resources when you can use your own. Consider doing things in-house where you can, especially expensive things. For instance if you need software for a particular task, the cost of having your in-house development team team write a simple program may be less than annually licensing third-party software.

Finally, another way to save on vendor costs is to barter or trade services or goods with other companies. Take care that neither of you is losing out in terms of an unequal trade. Similarly, look for mutually beneficial partnerships. For example, reduced prices from a vendor in exchange for positive online reviews, taking any legal issues about this into consideration. Effectively managing vendor relationships is part of cost management and can save your company big money.

SAVING ON FACILITY COSTS

It isn't always possible to move your work space, but there are ways that you can make the work space that you have work better for you. Saving on costs or even using it to earn extra income. Though it isn't always feasible to make changes, you can certainly try to maximize what you've got. In smaller spaces, change the layout. Adapt it to suit your needs by using repositionable walls or dividers as well as rearranging desks and other office items.

Where employees aren't in the office all the time like estate agents or sales teams, have them share office space. Consider having some employees work remotely. If you have extra space, subletting empty offices to other companies is a viable option. You can even rent out spaces when they're not being used such as conference rooms or other facilities for functions and events.

Consider selling old office equipment, furniture and decor items or donating them in exchange for a charitable tax receipt. It frees up space and helps helps the bottom line. Making your office more energy efficient can reduce the power cost. Simply ensure that all electronics and lights are turned off when the last person leaves the office. This includes things like copiers, computers and any other equipment that uses energy.

Lower the heat overnight, keeping it just warm enough for the next morning, but low enough to save on the heating bill. Obviously, you need to turn off equipment and lights when they're not in use, but you can also be energy efficient when they are. For example, opt for LED or fluorescent bulbs and use rechargeable batteries.

You can also purchase a printer that has an automatic sleep mode when not in use or look for products with the Energy Star label. To save when you're traveling, choose a company car or rental that is small and easy on gas. Making small changes to your services and office features goes a long way to help lower facility costs. Instead of buying new furniture, shop around for good quality second hand furniture.

Think about refinishing old furniture when it gets worn out, instead of throwing it away. If your office doesn't have clients coming in, fancy decor isn't necessary. You can save by having a small sparse office space, short on frills. Keep track of your maintenance and supply needs like your office dumpster schedule. If your trash is frequently emptied when it's only half full, then reduce the number of pickups.

You can also keep track of equipment signed out by employees, so missing inventory doesn't go unnoticed. And a final way to save on facilities is simply to reassess your needs. Move to a smaller space if possible or take the opportunity to renegotiate your rent to lower overall costs. While the space you work in may be predetermined, you can change and adjust it to make it more cost effective and efficient for you.

EXERCISE: SAVING YOUR COMPANY MONEY

In this exercise, you'll be required to identify ways you can contribute to saving money for your company. In this exercise, you'll demonstrate that you can:
- outline general cost management techniques
- recognize ways to save on business travel and entertainment costs
- identify ways to streamline supply and vendor costs, and
- distinguish ways to save on facility costs

Question

What are some examples of ways you can implement general cost-saving principles at work?

Options:

1. Make decisions as if you were spending your own money
2. Streamline inventory management
3. Reduce time spent on meetings and checking e-mail
4. Account for hidden costs such as tax, delivery charges, and installation fees when considering purchases
5. Work faster rather than better, and address quality issues later
6. See where you can add steps to processes to make them more comprehensive

Answer

Option 1: This option is correct. It can make a really positive difference to a company's bottom line if every employee makes business spending decisions responsibly, as if they were spending their own money

Option 2: This option is correct. Making a company's basic processes, such as inventory management, simpler and more efficient can yield significant cost savings.

Option 3: This option is correct. Reducing time spent on meetings and e-mail is one way to boost productivity, which is a key way to save costs.

Option 4: This option is correct. When making purchasing decisions, it's important to consider all the costs, not just the advertised sales price.

Option 5: This option is incorrect. Leaving quality issues for later is almost always more time-consuming and expensive than getting things right the first time.

Option 6: This option is incorrect. Making processes shorter and simpler, rather than more complex, tends to result in cost savings.

Question

What are some examples of ways to help cut down on company travel and entertainment costs?

Options:

1. Travel with colleagues, in the same car
2. Use price comparison sites to find the cheapest airfares
3. Use a company account for frequent flyer miles
4. Travel with the gear you need to work, such as a laptop and charger
5. Generally avoid travel packages; book flights and accommodation independently 6. Limit the number of clients you meet per business trip

Answer

Option 1: This option is correct. Traveling together by car is cheaper than traveling separately. Depending on distance, it may also be a cheap alternative to flying.

Option 2: This option is correct. Sites such as Expedia, Priceline, and Orbitz compare available prices of flights and hotel rooms and identify *the cheapest options.*

Option 3: *This option is correct. If employees fly often for business purposes, their frequent flyer miles can be used to defray the costs of business travel if collected on a company account.*

Option 4: *This option is correct. Business travel is expensive for a company because of lost productivity, as well as more direct costs. Ensuring you can work while you're away can help defray the cost.*

Option 5: *This option is incorrect. Travel packages often provide better value than booking flights, accommodation, and a rental car separately.*

Option 6: *This option is incorrect. If you have to travel to meet a particular client, it can save money to arrange meetings with additional clients in the same area. This makes it less likely you'll have to travel to the same location again in the near future.*

Question
What are some examples of ways to help reduce company supply costs?

Options:
1. Use free software for various business functions, such as accounting and inventory management
2. Look into leasing a photocopier instead of buying one
3. Configure printers and copiers to print on both sides of the page
4. Use cloud-based storage for documents
5. Source supplies from multiple vendors to keep them competing
6. When possible, use couriers instead of the mail

Answer

Option 1: *This option is correct. Seeking out free and discounted supplies, including items like software, can save a lot of money. A wide range of free software for business applications is available online.*

Option 2: *This option is correct. Especially for larger items, it may be more cost effective to rent equipment than to buy it. It's best to weigh the relative costs before making a decision.*

Option 3: *This option is correct. Changing how supplies are used – for* example, switching to double-sided printing to reduce the use of paper and ink or toner – can reduce waste and cut expenses.

Option 4: This option is correct. Distributing and storing data electronically using cloud-based storage is a good way to reduce supply costs. It eliminates the costs of paper, printing, and archiving of hard copies.

Option 5: This option is incorrect. The more you buy from one vendor, the more likely it is that your company will qualify for bulk discounts. Giving significant business to a single vendor can also increase your company's negotiating power with that vendor.

Option 6: This option is incorrect. Standard mail services are cheaper than courier services. Using the mail when it's appropriate to do so can save supply costs.

Question
What are examples of approaches to saving on vendor costs?
Options:
1. Negotiate for free deliveries
2. Regularly review your company's existing vendors
3. Periodically review all company insurance policies and call around for new quotes
4. Investigate the option of producing required content in-house instead of paying a third party to do it
5. 5. Secure long-term price agreements for computer hardware and peripherals 6. Always avoid outsourcing service functions, such as accounting

Answer

Option 1: This option is correct. It's vital to negotiate with vendors to secure the best possible deals. This can result in lower prices and other perks, such as free deliveries, longer payment terms, or extended warranties.

Option 2: This option is correct. Periodically review your company's existing relationships with vendors to determine if they're still in your company's best interests. It may be necessary to switch to an alternative vendor or to renegotiate current terms.

Option 3: This option is correct. Shopping around for insurance can lead to cheaper offers. It's also important to review existing policies to ensure your company isn't inadvertently paying for the same type of coverage more than once.

Option 4: This option is correct. It's important to weigh the relative costs of "make or buy" decisions. Sometimes it's much cheaper in the long run to produce a particular item or service in-house.

Option 5: This option is incorrect. It's best not to secure long-term agreements for items that are likely to become cheaper in the future, such as computer equipment.

Option 6: This option is incorrect. Sometimes it's cheaper and more effective to provide a service in-house, but this won't always be the case. It's important to weigh the costs, along with other advantages and disadvantages, of outsourcing in relation to handling functions in-house.

Question
What are some ways to save on facility costs?
Options:
1. Rent out spaces such as conference rooms when they're not in use
2. When buying office kitchen equipment, opt for energy-efficient models 3. Opt for second-hand office furniture
4. Sign the longest possible lease on office premises
5. Ensure employees get all their work done onsite instead of remotely
Answer
Option 1: This option is correct. Depending on the nature and location of your workspace, it may be possible to recoup some costs by renting out space when it's not in use. For example, it may be possible to rent out conference rooms for functions during off hours or on weekends.

Option 2: This option is correct. Energy-efficient printers, office kitchen equipment, and air conditioning units can help you save money over the long term.

Option 3: This option is correct. Provided it's of suitable quality, second-hand office furniture is likely to be much cheaper than new furniture. For example, you may be able to source furniture from going-out-

of-business sales.

Option 4: *This option is incorrect. It might not be in your company's best interests to sign a long lease. Its needs could change or lower rental prices may become available in the same or another area.*

Option 5: *This option is incorrect. Allowing employees to work from home can save a company money by reducing the space and facilities needed in an office.*

MANAGING WITH A COST-CONTROL MINDSET

Managing costs effectively is critical to business success and can help you avoid painful cuts. A business is unlikely to be as profitable as it could be if it doesn't adopt a cost-conscious culture. In this course, you'll learn how to identify cost management opportunities and how to get your team involved in the process. You'll also learn how you can save on personnel and overhead costs and about using practices like cost sharing and lean.

LOOKING FOR OPPORTUNITIES TO SAVE MONEY

Cost management is a difficult and often underappreciated part of being a manager. But when applied consistently, it reduces the need for sudden cost cutting. Cost management isn't about winning at the expense of customers or employees, and it doesn't have to mean lowering quality or unnecessarily laying off workers.

Effective cost management stems from having an effective cost leader who leads by example. Managers must take responsibility and ensure that effective cost management practices are in place, and team members need to be accountable, have cost targets and know who is responsible for each practice.

For cost management to work effectively, each department needs the right individual who is accountable for managing costs, hitting cost targets and providing progress reports. Put a feedback loop based on reliable data in place, so that members know where they stand with regards to their progress against targets. Your goal is to establish a culture of constant improvement focused on maximizing value and growth through low cost strategies.

It's important to know your expected cost trends, allowing you to budget accordingly and ensuring cost reductions and productivity increases. Bear in mind that any budgeting techniques you employ will only be effective if you are persistent and consistent in applying them. One useful technique is zero based budgeting.

It's a method where budgeting is started from scratch for every new project. It involves justifying costs from the ground up and considering alternatives and advantages that it provides a fresh perspective and encourages innovation because the budget doesn't assume anything. But beware, it can be time consuming and therefore potentially costly. It's important to understand where costs come from, the cost creators.

These can be direct or revenue producing costs, such as direct labor, materials or supplies necessary to produce the product or service or the indirect or overhead costs. *[Consider what drives each cost.]* Consider the drivers for each cost, what drives cost up or down. For example, the number of customers the service has or the number of products produced. But remember, you still have to spend money to make money.

Some costs are unavoidable and need to be factored into your budgeting. Think about costs of retaining and training employees, advertising products, travel to visit customers and product maintenance and support. These are necessary costs. To keep costs low, make individuals accountable for managing them instead of teams, so cost reduction efforts don't get lost in the shuffle and specific individuals are held accountable for achieving targets. T

here's always room for cost cutting in your organization. Look for expenses that aren't necessary and don't generate value for the company and make the needed cuts. Travel and entertainment, supplies, vendors and facilities are obvious places where costs can generally be reduced. Avoid unnecessary waste, both physical and time related whenever possible. Focus on getting quick results and cost reduction changes that generate the biggest impact.

Lead by example, following the same rules as your team. The goal is to create a culture that is conscious about the cost of literally everything.

GETTING YOUR TEAM INVOLVED IN SAVING

To make the right call when it comes to cost cutting, you need to know exactly what drives up costs in your company. One way to gather this information is to get the input of your front line employees. There's no better source of information than the employees who are figuratively in the trenches every day. They're in a position to identify where costs can be reduced that you just can't see.

One of the ways to get their input is to create a suggestion box. You can set up an email address or a messaging board dedicated to suggestions for employees' ideas. Encourage employees to expand upon their suggestions by providing things like cost and savings estimates or rollout plans. Develop a regular review process that includes a committee with employees representing all departments and employment levels.

Swap members out periodically to encourage involvement. A group brainstorming session is a good way to encourage employees to build off each other's ideas. Also seek out workers who are willing to take chances and try out new things. A low response rate is a real possibility when asking people to give feedback. Employees can be wary of expressing opinions *[Motivate employees to respond.]* and rocking the boat.

You'll get a better response if you motivate them by making the time and effort of offering suggestions worth it. Consider having a contest for suggestions and make it a fun team event. Put a reward system in place for suggestions that employee effective cost savings. Rewards can vary, including vacation days, bonuses or cash rewards.

Ensure that the reward fits the suggestion. In other words, if the employee suggestion saves the company millions of dollars, then they deserve more than a single vacation day or a minimal bonus. When suggestions are successful, celebrate the success and give credit where it is due. That will motivate increased participation the next time you sponsor this kind of initiative.

Employee contributions can make a significant impact when you're trying to cut down costs. You can ask employees to contribute by making even small changes, such as bringing a mug to work so that Styrofoam coffee cups aren't needed. Another strategy is to ask your employees how to reuse or repurpose old or aging equipment.

Ask them how they would reduce energy costs in the office. Similarly, employees need to know too that they're accountable for any company spending they do. Cost management is everyone's responsibility and everyone can be effective when they know where to apply the cuts. Employees have the most hands-on experience and can provide the most useful information. Get it, utilize it and reward it.

SAVING ON PERSONNEL COSTS

The employees of a company are often the single most expensive cost for a company. Moreover, people require office space and supplies and so on. Look for ways to reduce these costs when it makes sense for the organization. Meetings can be very effective, or they can waste a lot of time. Would an email update work just as well? Then do that instead. Have meetings only when necessary.

To maximize their effectiveness and increase productivity, always follow the same meeting format. Keep them on schedule by planning ahead and maintaining focus. Along those lines, if there are reports or documents being produced that no one reads, consider eliminating or streamlining them. Maybe, one consolidated monthly report will do instead of three weekly ones.

Think about office activities that are duplicated or unnecessary. Make sure your employees' assignments and tasks are clear and give them extra tasks within reason to encourage efficient work habits. An increase in worker productivity instead of hiring new people reduces the chances of layoffs. It's now possible for automation and technology to take over simple tasks from people and increase their productivity in other areas.

Think about the self checkout scanners at some grocery stores. Using technology where appropriate can really help reduce your costs. Can any tasks be replaced with automated processes? Other say forms that are being processed by humans that could be processed automatically instead with a new system or new code, use equipment and software to do what they were designed for.

If the machine is more efficient, let the machine do it. The person can be redeployed to perform more value added work. However, before buying new technologies, exhaust all other means of increasing productivity. Permanent full time staff are a meter cost for any organization.

To keep costs low, maintain a smaller number of permanent workers and hire temporary workers when there are natural peaks in workload. Short term and part time workers are a good way to fill brief gaps in employee coverage and great for workers looking for flexibility. Hiring interns is another great way to save on costs. Low salaries and no benefits payable, their hours are generally more flexible and they can bring fresh ideas and new perspectives. Consider advertising at local universities and colleges for freelance workers or get suggestions from your vendors.

Certain functions such as payroll may be candidates for outsourcing or you can use sub contractors with specialist knowledge in their fields. You'll save on the cost of training people in-house, but check on the costs versus savings of outsourcing regularly. It's not always the most cost effective solution. Employee layoffs are unpleasant, but maybe necessary for various reasons.

Perform regular performance appraisals and reduce staff when you have to. When larger scale layoffs are necessary, don't hide it from employees. Be upfront. Rumors cause stress and anxiety and reduce productivity. The best way to avoid layoffs is to avoid excessive hiring in the first place. Focus on increasing the productivity of your current employees first. Expand your thinking to view hiring as an investment and weigh the costs versus benefits. Make any payroll and promotion decisions carefully. Layoffs can incur multiple costs such as severance, unused vacation pay or even potential lawsuits.

Personnel costs can be expensive and the correct approach to managing personnel costs will save you money, particularly through task elimination, automation, alternative employment types and when necessary, layoffs.

SAVING ON ADVERTISING COSTS

In the current business environment, today's successful advertising strategy can be out of date tomorrow. You need to review it regularly. To start, focus on who your ideal customers are and target your advertising on them. This maximizes your return on investment or ROI. For example, an ad for a farm supply store placed in a general audience magazine isn't likely to generate results.

When you know who your ideal customer is, you'll know where to place your ads, so that your target customer sees it. Otherwise, you're wasting money. Likewise, paying for a commercial on TV when your target market has cut the cord and streams their entertainment is counterproductive. Do your research and find the best ways to hit your target. Customer surveys and market research are helpful.

While advertising is generally necessary and expensive, the way you advertise can save money in the long run. Narrow the scope of your advertising. Instead of an expensive and splashy ad campaign, choose more cost effective means of reaching your customers. Revamp your branding.

A clear logo is also a simple and effective way to advertise and remember too, advertising items with the company logo should be saved for advertising purposes that is outside the company. It's wasteful to use them in the office. Another way to save ad money is to make use of stock photos for visuals, instead of customizing your own.

Likewise, make full use of your in-house services to get the word out such as press releases and well placed editorials. Additionally, take the time to re-evaluate your mailing list to avoid duplicate mailings and clean out customers who have shown no interest. Lots of little savings add up to big cost cutting.

Further, eMarketing is a much more cost effective way to advertise than print and media ads. Use it wherever possible. Offer catalogs, flyers and other promotional material online. Encourage customers to sign up for emails, instead of making use of physical mailing lists. Make sure that people can find your website.

The site address should be clearly identifiable and included on things like ads, invoices, letterheads and e-mail footers. But there's no point of having a website if people don't see it. Your site needs to be engaging and offer content that will attract customers. To maximize website views, use electronic tactics such as search engine optimization, SEO, to make your company visible.

You also want to make sure that your company has a social media presence on platforms like Facebook, Twitter and Instagram and keep them up to date. Adding new content regularly so people will want to come back. Advertising is important to keep customers and gain new ones and the way you advertise can be cost effective, while still helping you reach your ideal audience.

SHARING COSTS AND COST STRATEGIES

Just as you learned in kindergarten, there is a value in sharing between departments, between companies and between business units. You can save big money by sharing costs and cost strategies within your organization *[Share costs with other departments.]* and with other organizations. Sharing costs requires coordination, like purchasing supplies in tandem with other departments to increase bulk order savings and to decrease shipping and delivery costs.

You can then split the cost of the coordinated purchase between the departments. You can also save on mailing costs by consolidating bulk mailing between departments. What if you have branches of the company spread out all over the country? Apply the same tactics. You can benefit from coordinating supply purchases by using a national rather than a local supplier, generating greater overall savings. It's one thing to coordinate purchases within a company, but what about between companies.

Consider forming alliances based on your strategic goals. For example, think of providing a discount in exchange for referrals, but remember when bartering, be sure you're aware of any tax or legal implications. When it comes to advertising, consider a joint promotion. For example, a purchase from company A gets customers a coupon for Company B. The two split the advertising costs.

For supply purchases, team up with other companies to buy in bulk. Sharing a building or other facility with another company provides a good opportunity to coordinate your supply restocking. This allows you to split the cost of both materials and delivery. You can also get cost savings advice from other companies who do business with you. They'll be inclined to help you if you are an important partner and they rely on you.

Think of vendors with whom you do significant business. How do they approach cost management? Can they offer helpful suggestions or advice? Another way you can share cost strategies is to share best practices between business units within the company. For example, consider the best practices of one store location in the chain that is going above and beyond in cost management.

Apply those practices to all of the other stores. Another example is extracting the best practices of one cost efficient office and re-applying them to the other offices or across regions. This tactic of sharing best practice can be most effective within the same company. However, you can also learn from companies that are in your same industry or even other industries. You can do some broad structural relative cost analysis of competitors to learn where your costs might be higher.

That can help you identify opportunities for improvement. You can also learn from companies and other industries who may have innovative ways of saving costs that you can apply in your business. Some of the greatest opportunities for innovation and improvement can come from looking outside your industry and applying the best ideas to your business. Sharing costs and cost strategies is an opportunity to to save money and provides opportunities to reassess your spending practices and behaviors.

SAVING MONEY BY IMPLEMENTING LEAN

Lean is a philosophy used in production that increases efficiency by cutting waste and simplifying processes. The goal is to create value for customers using as few resources as possible. The application of lean can have significant impact on a company's cost structure and improve its bottom line. Lean streamlines processes by removing waste in a continuous improvement initiative.

There are four steps in the process. Beginning with identifying the opportunity, this might involve preparing and training your employees to see opportunities for process improvement and cost reduction. Also, consider the value from the customer's perspective. The object is to identify existing improvement opportunities. The second step is to design an effective solution. This involves mapping the value stream to identify and cut activities that don't add value to the process or product.

When contemplating possible solutions, hold brainstorming sessions and encourage your employees to get involved. Lay out the current process and challenge every step. Employees are the closest to the process and their input can prove invaluable. Third is implementing the solution. This step involves deciding what to tackle in what order. Usually, the first order of business to tackle is the low hanging fruit. The issues and processes that are quick and cheap to address without any management involvement.

These issues produce results quickly and increase motivation to continue the process. The fourth and final step in lean is continuous improvement where employees take ownership for troubleshooting, allowing you to continue cutting waste, such as unnecessary labor and supply costs and incorporating further solutions as needed. Monitor processes to ensure that the improvements are sustained.

Kaizen means to change for the better. It's one of the tools that's used in implementing lean where small improvements are made throughout the value stream. It's best used for low hanging fruit and narrow scope problems that you understand well. It produces quick results and gets people on board, even those who are resistant to change, including cost reduction initiatives.

Kaizen includes tools for collecting and analyzing data, recommending improvements and implementing and monitoring changes. It's best used for issues that have a high impact and low effort. It's not as suitable for initiatives that are low impact and low effort or for very complex situations. High impact, high effort initiatives should be broken down into multiple Kaizen events. The Kaizen process has five main steps.

The first step is to identify the problem. This step involves understanding the goals, waste and planned benefits. The next step in the process is to gather and train the team. Here, you orientate the team to what you are doing and why you are doing it. Assemble a cross functional team, then plan events and create a schedule around them. Collecting and analyzing the data is the third step, followed by recommending improvements based on that analysis.

The final step is implementing and monitoring the changes. You begin by testing the proposed change and then implementing it once you're satisfied it will work. You then create a rollout plan, ensuring the team is trained and ready and monitoring their progress and performance against objectives. Lean processes are designed to cut waste and production time, saving your company money and helping you control your costs.

EXERCISE: MANAGING COSTS EFFECTIVELY

In this exercise, you're required to recognize efficient cost management practices for controlling organizational costs.
In this exercise, you'll demonstrate your ability to
- list strategies for managing costs
- recall how to engage your team in cost management efforts
- recognize tactics for managing personnel and advertising costs, and
- recall approaches to controlling costs through cost sharing and Lean

Question
Which examples reflect fundamental strategies for reviewing and reducing costs?
Options:
1. Communicate regularly with team members about costs and progress in meeting cost targets
2. Start budgeting processes from scratch every time
3. Identify all the factors that drive your company's current costs, such as number of employees and production volumes
4. Prioritize making the cost reductions that will yield the biggest savings for the least effort
5. Reduce the cost of budgeting processes by reusing existing budgets for new projects
6. Always focus first on reducing personnel costs, including training costs

COST CONSCIOUSNESS IN THE WORKPLACE

Answer

Option 1: *This option is correct. Effective cost management relies on proper feedback between managers and the team members who are accountable for controlling and managing costs effectively in practice.*

Option 2: *This option is correct. Zero-based budgeting, which involves budgeting from scratch every time, is a fundamental strategy for reducing costs. It ensures that costs are justified from the ground up and that new cost-cutting alternatives are considered.*

Option 3: *This option is correct. Effective cost management depends on a proper understanding of a company's current costs and what affects these costs. This is a starting point for identifying cost-cutting opportunities.*

Option 4: *This option is correct. Effective cost management relies on identifying opportunities for reducing costs and then prioritizing these properly. Generally, it's best to focus first on changes that will have the biggest impact but require the least time and effort to make.*

Option 5: *This option is incorrect. In general, zero-based budgeting – or budgeting from scratch every time – is more effective than reusing elements of existing budgets. Zero-based budgeting forces costs to be justified from the ground up and encourages consideration of new cost-cutting methods.*

Option 6: *This option is incorrect. It isn't always appropriate or cost-effective in the long run to cut personnel costs, such as training costs. Instead, it's vital to distinguish between necessary costs and those that may be eliminated or reduced without negatively affecting your company.*

Question
What are some examples of suitable ways to get cost-conscious input from employees?

Options:
1. Involve employees in reviewing submitted cost-saving suggestions
2. Give employees incentives, such as prizes, for submitting cost-saving suggestions
3. Ask employees to make small changes, such as reusing supplies,

to save money
4. Avoid giving individuals credit for cost-saving suggestions; make it clear that cost-saving is a team effort
5. Lead employees to believe that the company may not survive if they don't significantly cut costs

Answer

Option 1: *This option is correct. As well as encouraging employees to give suggestions, you should involve them in reviewing suggestions that are received. For example, set up a review committee that includes employees from different departments and levels, and regularly change its membership.*

Option 2: *This option is correct. Encourage employees to give suggestions by making it worth their while. For example, you might reward employees who give effective cost-cutting suggestions with prizes, vacation time, or cash rewards.*

Option 3: *This option is correct. It's a good idea to involve employees by asking them to make small cost-saving changes themselves. For example, ask them to reuse office supplies or bring their own mugs instead of using paper or Styrofoam cups at work.*

Option 4: *This option is incorrect. It's important to recognize and reward individuals who make valuable cost-cutting suggestions. This can help keep employees motivated and demonstrate that their ideas are valued.*

Option 5: *This option is incorrect. It's not appropriate to let employees think that their company is in financial difficulties or that they may face retrenchment unless this is really the case. Also, this is more likely to make employees seek jobs elsewhere than to take personal initiative in helping cut costs.*

Question

Which examples illustrate appropriate tactics for saving on personnel costs?

Options:
1. Make sure employees are given clear task instructions
2. Automate processes where possible
3. Investigate the option of hiring interns for certain positions

COST CONSCIOUSNESS IN THE WORKPLACE

4. Avoid excessive hiring and be cautious about payroll and promotion decisions 5. Offer compensation that's well below market rates
6. Reduce time and funds spent on performance appraisals

Answer

Option 1: *This option is correct. Giving employees clear instructions for completing tasks, as well as ensuring they're assigned enough work, improves productivity. In turn, this may make it unnecessary to hire more staff or to institute layoffs. Clear task guidelines will also help cut down on unnecessarily duplicated tasks.*

Option 2: *This option is correct. Technology that automates tasks may replace the need for certain staff members or make existing staff members more productive. This translates into savings on personnel costs.*

Option 3: *This option is correct. Interns – as well as temporary, part-time, and freelance workers – can save on the costs of full-time personnel. Interns typically receive low wages and no benefits, but are often motivated to work hard and may contribute up-to-date industry knowledge and ideas.*

Option 4: *This option is correct. Focus on increasing the productivity of existing staff members before considering hiring new workers. Being conservative about promotions and pay increases can also prevent overspending on personnel and help avoid the need for layoffs.*

Option 5: *This option is incorrect. If personnel aren't offered competitive compensation, high performers are unlikely to accept positions or stay with the company.*

Option 6: *This option is incorrect. It's important to conduct regular performance appraisals to identify personnel who are performing poorly. Steps can then be taken to improve productivity or lay off underperforming workers.*

Question

What are some effective approaches to reducing marketing and advertising costs?

Options:

1. Determine your company's ideal customers and focus advertising on them

2. Opt for advertising that has limited reach but offers a high return on investment
   3. Use search engine optimization and appealing web site content to attract customers
   4. Prioritize television and radio marketing, which reach the broadest audiences
   5. Spend the most on local advertising

Answer

Option 1: This option is correct. Rather than trying to advertise to everyone, aim to reach those most likely to buy your products or services. The more targeted marketing is, the higher the return it provides.

Option 2: This option is correct. A good way to save costs is to narrow the scope of your advertising. Focus on media and techniques that reach fewer people and are therefore cheaper, but that are properly targeted and have a high success rate.

Option 3: This option is correct. Digital marketing can be much cheaper than other types of marketing, especially if companies manage some or all of their online content themselves.

Option 4: This option is incorrect. To reduce costs, aim to narrow the scope of your advertising. Instead of trying to reach the biggest possible audience, make your marketing more targeted so it reaches only those most likely to buy your company's products or services.

Option 5: This option is incorrect. The ideal marketing strategy will depend on the nature and locations of your company's target markets.

Question

What are some ways to effectively reduce costs by working with other groups?

Options:
   1. Coordinate supply purchases between company branches
   2. Partner with another company to buy supplies in bulk
   3. Have business units share effective cost-cutting practices
   4. Have different departments order supplies from different vendors, to foster competition

5. Implement exactly the same cost-cutting practices as your most successful competitor

Answer

Option 1: *This option is correct. If multiple branches, or even multiple divisions at a single branch, combine their orders for supplies, they're more likely to benefit from bulk discounts.*

Option 2: *This option is correct. Bulk purchases typically qualify for discounts. Multiple companies can collaborate to quality for discounts and then split the savings.*

Option 3: *This option is correct. Within a company, it's useful for business units – including particular branches and departments – to share best practices for cutting costs. They face similar types of expenses and requirements, and so are often in a position to benefit from similar strategies.*

Option 4: *This option is incorrect. It's generally more cost-effective to have departments combine their orders. This means they're more likely to qualify for bulk purchase discounts. Also, one delivery is cheaper than multiple, separate deliveries.*

Option 5: *This option is incorrect. Different companies operate differently and measure success in different ways. Even if you could identify all of a competitor's cost-cutting practices, it's unlikely it would make sense for your company to copy them exactly.*

Question

Implementing the Lean process can significantly reduce costs. Sequence the stages in an example of the Lean process.

Options:
1. Recognize automation of form processing as a way to save time and costs
2. Customize simple software for automating form processing

3. Configure team members' systems with new software for automating form processing
4. Ask team members to keep suggesting ways to make form submissions and processing more efficient

Answer

Recognize automation of form processing as a way to save time and costs is ranked. Identifying an opportunity for improvement – such as a way to boost productivity and cut costs – is the first step in the Lean process.

Customize simple software for automating form processing is ranked. Once you've identified an opportunity for improvement, the next step – step two – is to design a solution that lets you make use of the opportunity. For example, this might involve customizing software, modifying an existing process, or making some other change.

Configure team members' systems with new software for automating form processing is ranked. The third step of the Lean process is implementing the solution you've designed. For example, this might involve setting up systems and training staff members.

Ask team members to keep suggesting ways to make form submissions and processing more efficient is ranked. The fourth and final step of a Lean process is implementing continuous improvements. Rather than making a change and just accepting the new status quo, continue striving for better, more cost-effective solutions. One way to do this is to solicit suggestions and input from team members.

www.ingramcontent.com/pod-product-compliance
Lightning Source LLC
Chambersburg PA
CBHW072238230526
45466CB00025B/2112